TESS WHITEHURST
ARTWORK BY MÉLANIE DELON

THE ORACLE OF THE

VAMPIRE
FAE

*FIERCE FEMININE WISDOM
FROM THE BAOBHAN SITH*

THE ORACLE OF THE VAMPIRE FAE
Fierce Feminine Wisdom from the Baobhan Sith

Copyright © 2026 Tess Whitehurst
Artwork Copyright © 2026 Mélanie Delon

All rights reserved. Except for personal use, no part of these cards or this book may be reproduced, in whole or in part, without written permission from the publisher. These cards are for spiritual and emotional guidance only and are not a substitute for medical advice or treatment. The author's views, within and beyond this publication, do not necessarily reflect those of the publisher. We respectfully request that this content not be used to train AI-generative models or machine learning systems without the publisher's written consent.

Published by Blue Angel Publishing®
10 Trafford Court, Wheelers Hill,
Victoria, Australia 3150
E-mail: info@blueangelonline.com
Website: www.blueangelonline.com

Edited by Jules Sutherland & Peter Loupelis

Blue Angel is a registered trademark of Blue Angel Gallery Pty Ltd.

ISBN: 978-1-922574-49-7

Printed on sustainably sourced paper,
with soy-based inks.

ENTER THE LAIR OF THE VAMPIRE FAE 7

HOW TO PREPARE YOUR DECK FOR USE 9
HOW TO DO A READING WITH *THE ORACLE OF THE VAMPIRE FAE* 10

THE CARDS

1. FOREVER FREE 14
2. THE ALCHEMY OF PASSION 16
3. HEIRESS 18
4. DESTINY ACKNOWLEDGED 20
5. JADED HEART 22
6. VULNERABLE WARRIOR 24
7. TURNING POINT 26
8. WOUNDED DIVA 28
9. LOVE AND LET GO 30
10. WILD MEDICINE 32
11. RADIANT WITCH 34
12. ELITE SOLDIER 36
13. CLAIM THE THRONE 38
14. INITIATION 40
15. FEED THE SPIRIT 42
16. MOONLIGHT ELIXIR 44
17. NEW REGIME 46
18. RICHES OF GAIA 48
19. DIVINE IDENTITY 50
20. DESPERATE FOR DECEPTION 52
21. YOUR OWN WORLD 54
22. MAKE A WISH 56
23. SEE BEYOND 58
24. FATE INTO DESTINY 60

25. BEYOND DEATH 62
26. AKASHIC UNWEAVING 64
27. AMBASSADOR 66
28. MIDWINTER 68
29. NOT A SINNER 70
30. PROTECTIVE VEIL 72
31. FRESH AIR 74
32. ENTITLED TO SHINE 76
33. DARK JEWEL 78
34. LADY IN WHITE 80
35. THE MORRIGAN 82
36. ANCESTOR MAGIC 84
37. VISIONARY 86
38. ENLIST THE FETCH 88
39. LIGHT THE NIGHT 90
40. RULE WITH EASE 92
41. BEAUTIFUL NIGHTMARE 94
42. A GOOD DAY TO DIE 96
43. THE END IS THE BEGINNING 98
44. WELCOME THE STORM 100
45. ALCHEMY 102
46. QUEEN 104
47. ASSASSIN 106
48. STEADFAST PROTECTOR 108
49. A NEW DAY 110
50. ASK AND KNOW 112
51. WINDS OF CHANGE 114
52. EYE OF THE STORM 116

ABOUT THE AUTHOR 119
ABOUT THE ARTIST 121

ENTER THE LAIR OF
THE VAMPIRE FAE

T HIS ORACLE CHANNELS THE WISDOM OF THE majestic Scottish race of vampiric faeries called the *baobhan sith* (pronounced "boe-bun-SHEE"). To humans, the *baobhan sith* appear most often as beautiful women with an otherworldly radiance. Their beauty serves them well in catching their prey, as their meal of choice is the blood and flesh of adulterous, abusive, and controlling men. (But they are happy to make a snack of any human of any gender who mistreats their partner or otherwise misuses their privilege or power.)

The *baobhan sith* are shapeshifters. When they are not in their most well-known form as gorgeous female humans, they can be seen running through moonlit forests as wolves and flying through the starry night as ravens or crows. Sometimes, while in their human shape, they choose to walk on hooves instead of feet.

While it may seem vicious to feed on human flesh, consider that many of us feed on the flesh of other animals daily. One important distinction the vampire fae would like to point out is that the animals humans eat are innocent. In contrast, the *baobhan sith* feast on abusers and batterers: those who willfully hurt others through domination and manipulation.

The *baobhan sith* are alchemists. They take old, worn-out conditions and beliefs and transform them into blinding power and beauty. They help you dismantle oppressive relationships, destroy unhealthy dynamics, and move out of living situations that keep you feeling stuck and small. They assist you in transforming from victim to victor, from captive to queen.

What are the origins of the *baobhan sith*? They were born into this world in response to a need. Whenever one human seeks to hurt, control, or exploit another under the false moniker of protection or love, an energetic vacuum is created and an etheric imbalance is formed. But as the saying goes, nature abhors a vacuum. And so the *baobhan sith* arose naturally from this imbalance to restore equilibrium through immaculate protection and justice.

The words in this guidebook are transcribed and arranged by me, the author — Tess Whitehurst. But the energy and essence of the wisdom are directly from the *baobhan sith*. The first few lines in each card description encapsulate the wisdom in a pure and distilled form. After that, you will find finely tuned guidance from the vampire fae to encourage you, bolster you, and help you understand how to put the wisdom to use.

Work with *The Oracle of the Vampire Fae* whenever you feel guided to, but particularly when you seek to shore up your spiritual defenses, set and enforce your boundaries, get out of a painful or unhealthy relationship, find your voice, heal your heart, or otherwise reclaim your personal power. Anytime you have forgotten your innate worthiness and beauty, or you feel anxious or unsafe, the *baobhan sith* are powerful allies to invoke.

HOW TO PREPARE YOUR DECK FOR USE

Light a red candle. Hold the cards in both hands. Close your eyes, relax, and take some deep breaths. Focus on the cards and send energy into them through your hands. Imagine the cards being filled with bright golden light. Enlist the support of these powerful spirits by saying:

Vampire faeries, baobhan sith, I invoke you.
As I consult these cards, help me to see and to know.
May I fully claim, own, and wield my power.
May I be the authority in my own life,
and always, always be free.
You are most kind.

Continue to hold the cards as you feel your personal energy and consciousness merging with the energy and wisdom of the deck. Sense the uniquely empowering magic of the imagery, and say, "You are most kind" to the vampire fae once again. (This phrasing is agreeable to the fae. Try to avoid using "please" or "thank you," for it is considered rude in their realm.)

HOW TO DO A READING WITH *THE ORACLE OF THE VAMPIRE FAE*

To do a reading, hold the deck in both hands. Relax and center your body and mind by closing your eyes and taking some deep breaths. Then ask for guidance in the form of a "You are most kind to___" statement. For example, you might ask for general guidance by saying something like, "You are most kind to show me what it will most benefit me to know now." Or, you can request specific guidance by saying something like, "You are most kind to offer me the wisdom that will best support me with regard to [this particular challenge or issue]."

Shuffle the cards in any way you choose. Then, from anywhere in the deck, draw one to three cards. Don't think too much about this step or take too long with it. Just draw, and trust that the card or cards you select will always be just right for you now.

For a one-card reading, the message is straightforward. It is the succinct and overriding answer to your question.

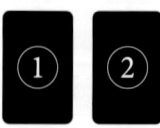

For a two-card reading, the first card offers insight into what you are dealing with and what changes are happening for you now. The second card provides insight and advice on what to do.

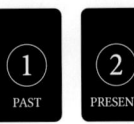

For a three-card reading, Card One is where you've been and the factors leading up to your present issue or challenge. Card Two is where you are now and what you're in the middle of. Card Three is where you are going, and what will most benefit you to keep in mind moving forward.

After laying out your card or cards, before turning to the corresponding pages in the guidebook, take some time to simply observe the image(s) and the card title(s) underneath. Let the magic of the image absorb into your spirit and soul. Let the attitude and posture of the vampire fae in the image wash over and through you, fortifying your power and resolve. You don't need to figure anything out at this point. Allow this to be an energy healing that goes beyond words and the linear-thinking mind.

Then, turn to the guidance in the book for each card you have drawn. Read slowly, without rushing the process. Notice any words or phrases that stand out to you, and be alert to any intuitive hits about how the guidance applies to your question, issue, or challenge. Allow your inner wisdom to be illuminated and your way forward to be clear.

The *baobhan sith* are indeed fearsome, but don't be afraid. They are fierce, but so are you. You are a feral force of nature and a ferocious queen of the night. Let them remind you.

THE CARDS

1. FOREVER FREE

Assert your independence. Free yourself from an oppressive relationship or life condition. You have more authority than you are presently wielding.

LIKE AN APEX PREDATOR, DO NOT ALLOW YOURSELF TO BE HUNTED, CAPTURED, OR TAMED.

To take back your power, it will help to see every relationship in your life as a choice you are making. If you stay, it's because you are choosing to stay. You are the one perpetuating your commitments, contracts, and unspoken agreements. Even if you are not choosing how you are treated, you are choosing who you spend time with, how you respond to them, and the responsibilities you adopt and fulfill.

If it seems like others are making these choices for you,

now is the time to reclaim the authority that is intrinsically yours.

This may be a message about leaving or significantly altering a relationship, living situation, or job, or it may simply be a reminder that all choices in your life are yours to make. Take back your power and your freedom. You are beholden to no one. You are no one's plaything or pet.

Right now, inwardly or aloud, say to yourself decisively: "I call the shots. I set my boundaries. And I enforce them." Repeat it until you believe it all the way down to your bones. This is an inner shift that you can make this very moment. No fanfare or grand announcements required.

The image on the card is a mirror of the character of your own soul, which is forever wild, powerful, and free. Relax your body, clear your mind, gaze at the image, and feel your true nature reawaken within.

Now that you remember yourself as the independent warrior you are, how has your perspective shifted? What do you want? What do you reject? What conditions suit you, and what will you no longer tolerate? From this place of incorruptible, indestructible, absolute inner authority, how will you proceed?

Storms rage. Lightning flashes. Giant ocean waves crash against the shore. In just the same way, your autonomy is a stunning natural force that should not and cannot be contained.

Your path forward is a path that only you can recognize or detect. Your freedom will serve as an instinctual inner compass that will show you the way.

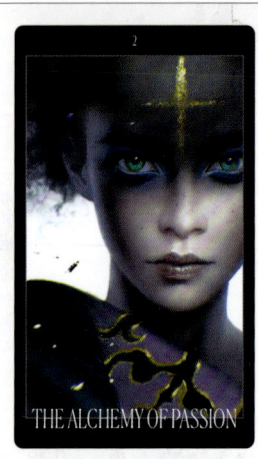

TAP INTO YOUR FIERCE INNER FIRE.

2. THE ALCHEMY OF PASSION

Channel your emotion into action. Hunt down the fire within you and stoke it. Uncover hidden feelings and let them flow.

Transform your empathy and compassion into power.

When your impulse to create positive change is ignored or denied, it festers. Honor your feelings by channeling them into constructive action or activism.

When you feel your feelings related to suffering and injustice, your righteous indignation will become a radiant, cleansing fire — this is the divine flame that fuels the hearts of the *baobhan sith*. It is a fire that stokes the flames of our beauty and resilience, and it will do the same for you.

Your passion to help bring about greater justice, fairness, and equality may be obvious and easily accessible, or you could be hiding it somewhere — concealing it with logic, humor, busyness, self-criticism, or a desire to be "good" or "nice."

If you have been mistreated in the past, or if you are being mistreated now, are you making excuses for the person or group who has instigated this mistreatment? Are you saying to yourself, "They don't realize," or "They don't mean it," or "They couldn't help it because they were hurt too"? Or are you telling yourself that you don't really care about it anymore, or you're over it, or you never cared about it in the first place?

End this nonsense. Simper, deny, and hide no more. Acknowledge, feel, and express your feelings so that you may truly let them go.

There is hidden power here. Find the feelings, and feel them, and you will free up the power. Think of it like old rotting wood that you are lighting up with cleansing, sparkling fire and light.

You can illuminate your true feelings by breathing deeply and consciously. Feel the breath moving energy around your body, opening up the hidden and stuck places in your energy field where your emotion may be furtively lodged.

Once you locate the fiery fuel for change, feel it. Breathe into it. Encourage the fire and let it burn. Cry if you need to, or dance, or go for a run. Let the feelings move through your body like flames. Activate the energy and let it flow. Know what you desire to change, and just how you want to change it. Then, decisively and without apology, proceed.

CLAIM YOUR BIRTHRIGHT.

3. HEIRESS

OPEN TO YOUR DIVINE INHERITANCE. YOU ARE ENTITLED TO RECEIVE MORE WEALTH THAN YOU HAVE PREVIOUSLY EXPECTED. ALLOW YOUR RICHES TO FLOW IN.

You are the heir to a vast and endless fortune: born to be elegant, lucky, and rich.

In the past, you may have believed that before you can experience the abundance you desire, you must get multiple degrees, build up your resume, heal all your old issues, and change all your limiting beliefs. But what if there are no prerequisites to your prosperity? What if your riches are here for you now, already, and are just waiting for you to recognize them, demand them, and gather them to you?

Money is energy, and while it may correlate to behaviors and conditions in the physical world, in truth, it transcends and precedes them. In other words, to claim your inheritance, you don't have to start with any external quality or condition. You can work your magic. You can start with expecting and believing, and watch avenues of abundance open and generous windfalls appear.

Do your best to let go of tension in your body and mind. Then, simply be willing to own the role that has been yours since the beginning — daughter of the wild night, beloved by the vampire fae, undisputed heiress to unlimited stockpiles of wealth.

To open to your true nature as heiress, look for the luxury that's present in your life, and celebrate all the many blessings you already have. Luxury begets luxury. By reveling in the wealth that's already yours, you will free up even more of your fortune. The more often you do this, the more momentum you will activate, and the more riches will come flowing and tumbling in.

You do not need to do anything special to deserve the wealth that is yours by divine right. It is intrinsic to you. Like your fingerprints or the color of your eyes, it is a natural aspect of who you are. You are entitled to vast riches, and we the vampire fae want you to know it in every fiber of your being. Relax, breathe, believe, and receive.

IGNORE YOUR DESTINY NO LONGER.

4. DESTINY ACKNOWLEDGED

Embrace your divinely appointed role. Acknowledge what you know you must do. Surrender all old stories about your insignificance and step into your predestined role as healer, warrior, and queen.

Your sacred role may take the form of a job, calling, or career path. But it begins on the internal plane. Though it is intensely significant, it may or may not be obvious to the world. All your interactions, actions, and communications can be channeled for its use.

You have unique spiritual talents and abilities that allow you to fight for what is beautiful, just, and true. In short, you are a warrior priestess. You have elected to be born into this life to act as an agent of feminine power.

The actions you take in response to acknowledging your destiny may take many forms. But if you relax, look within, and consult your inner guidance system, you will know how to proceed.

You may be guided to master a particular form of therapy, such as psychology, herbal healing, or conventional Western medicine. You might feel drawn to learn about and practice an occult or intuitive art, such as tarot, astrology, or feng shui. But you may also desire to channel your sacred work into your everyday interactions with friends, acquaintances, and loved ones. You may even express your role through a seemingly unrelated career, such as fashion, law, or real estate. Truly, anything can be a vehicle for your feminist mission. The form your work takes is less important than the intention you bring to it.

You are already aware of this destiny. For some time now, it has been asking for your acknowledgment through nudges and intuitive hits. Disregard and downplay these messages no longer. Embrace and embody your destiny without any further delay.

5. JADED HEART

Your heart has closed in response to past pain or betrayal. This is constricting your pleasure and possibly causing you to see friends as enemies and enemies as friends. Be courageous enough to open your heart, and you will rediscover your joy.

GUARDING YOUR HEART IS DRAINING YOUR ALIVENESS.

When you are hurt, it can be as if your fiery heart turns to ice. This cuts you off not just from those who would harm you, but also from allies and potential allies, and even from yourself. Your joy becomes fully or partially frozen. You can't totally perceive or understand your own feelings, and you are unable to revel in the wild freedom that is your true nature.

Unchain and unburden your heart. Liberate your feral spirit. Refuse to live in fear for one moment longer. Rediscover your sense of possibility. Be curious about and open to those you love, as well as potential lovers and friends. And remember that life is magical.

Place one hand on your heart and one hand on your belly. Send yourself love through your hands, and remind yourself that you are a majestic and powerful creature, born to run through the forest under the full moon at night. Breathe deeply and consciously. If painful emotions come up, let them strengthen and bolster you. Breathe into them as if you are stoking a raging fire. With each breath, feel more and more open, more and more powerful, more and more alive.

When a heart opens after it has been closed, there is often pain. But it will not last forever. It is only passing through. Cry if you need to. Feel and sense the pain making you stronger. And then allow yourself to see when, why, and how your heart decided to close. Who or what in your current life experience have you shut out? It could be a partner, a friend, a family member, or a formerly cherished activity or goal. It could be a potential partnership or alliance. It could even be yourself. Does it make sense to open up to this person or condition? Or perhaps, from this place of empowered clarity, you will realize it is time to set a boundary, speak a truth, or say goodbye.

BARE YOUR SOUL AND BREATHE INTO PAIN.

6. VULNERABLE WARRIOR

TRUE FIERCENESS REQUIRES VULNERABILITY. ALL BEINGS SUFFER. BE WILLING TO FEEL YOUR SUFFERING, AND YOU WILL TRANSCEND THE LIMITATIONS OF FEAR.

It is a myth that emotional armor will protect you from being manipulated or used. In fact, you will take better care of yourself when you are attuned to the subtleties of your heart's wisdom.

Every day, take some time to relax your body and mind. Breathe consciously, let your body relax, and awaken your sensitivity. Choose to be yourself fully, and to bravely be seen and known for who you are.

Being true to yourself is a superpower. So, bring your

assertiveness online and speak your truth plainly. This will steer you in the direction of your dreams. It will illuminate whom you do and do not want to spend time with, and who is worthy of your trust. It will activate your intuition and help you to know just what to do.

No matter how fierce you may be, you are also capable of great tenderness and loving connection, and everyone needs to experience these things to thrive. Even a vampire needs to love and be loved. Divest yourself of your armor, embody receptive openness, and share your true self with the world.

Of course, you are still a formidable force. And you can keep your defenses at the ready for when you need them. Just remember that without opening yourself up to rejection and disappointment, you may never lose, but you will also never win. Living authentically, passionately, and beautifully will always require risk.

Find your courage. Bare your heart. Let yourself be seen. Play it safe at your peril — risking shame and failure is the only path to glorious success.

THE TIME IS NOW.

7. TURNING POINT

THIS IS A TURNING POINT. DON'T HESITATE. TAKE DECISIVE ACTION AND FREE YOURSELF FROM PAST CHALLENGES.

You can't go on like this. You must act decisively, free your spirit, and bring about positive change.

The story that is now playing out for you has reached or is about to reach a transformative moment of truth. Stop running from what you know, and from what you know you need to do. Speak up for yourself and stand up for yourself. Take bold action and overcome your fear.

The message of this card may be completely obvious to you. But if you don't know what it's about, ask yourself: "In what way do I feel disempowered in this situation or at this moment? Who or what do I perceive as tormenting or oppressing me, keeping me down, or holding me in thrall?"

Once you have your answer, remind yourself that the only person smack in the middle of your life experience is you. You are the primary power and motivating force. Of course there will be other factors—people, intentions, and conditions—that play a role in your experience, but you always hold the ultimate authority and seniority about where you will be, what you will do, and whom you will be with.

Embody this authority now by saying a clear yes to what you want and no to what you don't want. Wield this simple yet absolute power on both inner and outer planes.

You may need to brave some temporary discomfort to get to a better place. But it will be worth it. So decide on a bold action and take it. Make the travel arrangements, have the conversation, withstand the uncertainty, and unsettle the status quo. You can't stay in your comfort zone anyway, because your comfort zone has long since ceased to be comfortable.

If you feel desperate, embrace your desperation. Breathe into it and use it as fuel for the cleansing fire of change.

You don't need to go it alone. Find someone you trust, and ask for any help you need. But don't delay for another moment. Now is the time to get free.

YOUR AGONY HAS NOT RUINED YOU — IT HAS MADE YOU BEAUTIFUL.

8. WOUNDED DIVA

THERE IS ALCHEMY IN PAIN. GREAT ART IS BORN FROM PROFOUND SUFFERING. OWN YOUR TRAUMA, YOUR ANGER, AND YOUR HEARTBREAK. CHANNEL YOUR EMOTIONS INTO CREATIVITY, AND YOUR MAGIC WILL COME ALIVE.

Your unique wounding has conferred special gifts and perspectives that your soul dearly wants and needs to express.

If you're not sure what form of creativity to practice, choose the one that feels frightening in the most exciting possible way. Decide where and when you will do it. And then show up for it, again and again.

And do it soon! The longer you wait, the more this vital current of creative energy will be congested within you, which will perpetuate stagnation and discomfort. So don't worry too much about selecting just the right medium of expression. Just start. In time, and with the wisdom of experience, you can always pivot into a new discipline or avenue of self-expression.

This is not a message about becoming a famous artist, or impressing people, or being the very best at something (although you will certainly, in the process, achieve some degree of mastery over your craft). This is a simple message that you absolutely must express yourself creatively and prolifically, starting now.

Every medium of creativity is a spiritual discipline and healing path. Employ visual, somatic, auditory, or performance art now to heal from trauma, establish your confidence, and find your voice.

All emotions, stories, and experiences are fuel for the creative fire. If you've been concealing something out of shame, pull it out of the darkness and throw it on the flames. Creativity is alchemy. It can be employed to continuously burn away the rotting wood and heavy lead of your hardship, transforming it into spun gold and sparkling light.

Transcend your fear and find your courage. Ignite your aching heart and make it spark and glow for the world to see. It is a precious and vital beauty that is born from pain.

RISE ABOVE THE PAST AND BE FREE.

9. LOVE AND LET GO

Banish that which no longer serves you. Close the door on a relationship, pattern, or condition. Move onwards and upwards to an empowered new way of being.

Life is both an endless stream of new experiences and a continuous series of goodbyes. To open up to the new, you must let go of the old: the beliefs and dynamics that limit you, as well as the seasons and situations that naturally and inevitably pass away.

Breathe, relax deeply, cut the cords, and bid farewell.

Jobs end, dreams evaporate, loved ones transition out of this life experience, and children grow up and move away. Stop fighting the change and gracefully flow with it instead. Acknowledge, then intentionally release whatever has recently made its exit from your life experience or whatever is making its exit now.

Feel your emotions in any way that feels appropriate and right. Cry, grieve, rage, create art, clear out old belongings related to the old condition, perform a ritual of gratitude, or hold a bittersweet celebration of what was.

If you're hanging on to any guilt or remorse about this ending or the way it played out, let it go. You did what you could and what felt right to you at the time, and that's all you can ever do. Forgive yourself for any perceived mistakes, let regret transform into simple heartache, and then feel that heartache bravely so you can let it move through like a weather pattern and evaporate.

You can't change the past anyway, so you might as well let go of it and let it be. In turn, this will help you to heal deeply, open to the present moment, and welcome in your beautiful future.

Feel your feelings, cut the cords, and say goodbye. Let go of the past, take back your power, and know that you have all you need within you to thrive.

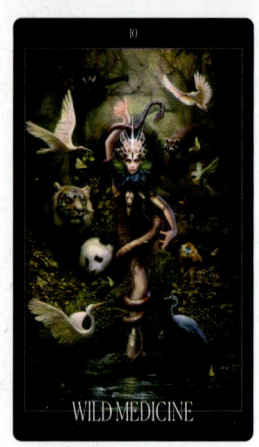

REDISCOVER YOUR WILD MAGIC.

10. WILD MEDICINE

ALLOW THE EARTH TO ENLIVEN, EMPOWER, AND INSPIRE YOU. DRAW UPON THE WISDOM OF ANIMALS AND THE ENERGY OF THE LAND. ACCESS DEEP HEALING AND VAST PERSONAL POWER.

Use your intuition to recalibrate your approach. Begin by gazing at the image before you. Which of the animals stands out to you? Which one glows, or speaks to you, or inspires you the most? Take your time and look closely. You may be surprised by the animal you choose.

Now, ask yourself: "Why did I choose this creature? What energy am I picking up on when I look at it? What quality, emotion, or vibration does this animal impart?"

Once you find your own answers to these questions, consider the following. A butterfly will likely indicate a transformation of some kind. A sea bird might be about purifying your energy or getting yourself free. The parrot: communication. The tiger: fierce power. The panda: abundance, wisdom, and luck. One or both of the monkeys could be about using your intelligence, skill, and creative wiles. The snake: Divine Feminine power or physical healing. The raccoon: magic and resourcefulness. The alligator might be a message about merging with nature and lying low, perhaps quietly knowing that you can immediately defend yourself whenever the need may arise.

Also consider the rich lushness of the ecosystem here: the sparkling water, the soil, the greenery, and the thick forest providing food, oxygen, and shade. Even if you're indoors, breathe, relax, and connect with the energy of the earth beneath you. Allow yourself to receive an infusion of steadying support.

As soon as you can, take yourself to a serene natural setting and stand on the earth. Connect with the elements and the landscape. Listen to the birds, gaze at the plants, and feel the breeze on your skin. In the three-dimensional world, notice any plants or animals that seem to have messages for you, and listen to those messages. Receive them not as language so much as waves of energy that transform your brainwaves, molecules, and cells. Feel your body and energy field fill up with the bolstering, balancing light of the earth.

Speak to the animals and commune with the planet. Remember that you are a wild creature yourself, and let that remembering heal you, guide you, and set you free.

UNLEASH YOUR BEAUTY.

11. RADIANT WITCH

Be shockingly and dangerously gorgeous. Stoke your glow as a magical act. Burnish your loveliness, luxuriate in your splendor, and dance gracefully with the unique magic of who you are.

Your culture tells you vicious lies about what it means to be beautiful. Stop believing them. And begin, this moment, to unapologetically wield your monstrous sensuality and charm.

Your beauty is unlike anyone else's, as is your style. When you relate to your body like the precious vessel it is, you will activate your intrinsic personal power and wield the full depth and breadth of your authority.

Take a moment to relax and breathe. When you feel awake and attuned to your body, listen deeply to what health, style, and beauty practices will most nourish and support you now. It might be time for a spa treatment, a salon visit, or some conscious self-care. You may discover that your self-adornment practice or makeup routine could use a shake-up, or perhaps it's time to make conscious additions to your wardrobe that help you feel like the fabulous creature you are.

You can calibrate and fine-tune your relationship with your beauty by getting rid of clothes and accessories that you no longer love, or that you never loved in the first place. You may also want to get rid of the old lotions, potions, and other cosmetics that you don't value or use.

This could also be a message about tending to the inner health that nourishes your outer splendor. Perhaps you will benefit from drinking more water, eating more vegetables, going for daily walks in the fresh air, getting more sleep, meditating, or stretching in the mornings before you get busy with your daily routine. On the other hand, perhaps you need to play more — to let loose, dance sensually, and laugh wildly in the night.

When you follow your body's guidance to stoke your inner well-being and radiate your unique personal essence and glow, you will boost your lifeforce energy, elevate your vibration, and more easily attract the conditions you desire.

Stop hiding your gorgeousness and downplaying your brilliance. Let your formidable beauty and magic burn brightly for the world to see. Ignite your inspiration and bless the world with your fire and light.

CONQUER AND WIN.

12. ELITE SOLDIER

SHORE UP YOUR COURAGE AND BE THE ELITE SOLDIER YOU ARE IN TRUTH. CALL UPON ALL THE RESILIENCE, WISDOM, SKILL, AND AUTHORITY YOU WERE BORN WITH. WIELD THE WISDOM AND MASTERY YOU HAVE GAINED THROUGH PAST STRUGGLE AND PAIN.

We would not wish your past challenges upon you. But through them, you have learned to adapt, survive, and even thrive.

Like the vampire fae in this image, be simultaneously fierce and relaxed. Even as you ride to battle, be secure in your power: at peace with yourself and the world. While you may not be adversarial by nature, there are times when you need to fight for things like justice, your own independence, and the people and animals you love.

You need not bluster or even break a sweat. But do embody the vicious fierceness that will serve you in battle. Be quiet, confident, and graceful even as your heart burns with righteous rage. Channel that rage toward gaining back your territory, establishing your terms, and vanquishing your inner and outer foes.

We the vampire fae find that wielding such understated and streamlined mastery can be fun. Elite warriors, also, have been known to experience delicious pleasure as they move through a battlefield with grace.

If you feel exhausted, fried, or overwhelmed, there is a vast store of divine energy accessible to you. Relax your body and mind, breathe deeply, and access the invigorating fire at your heart.

Set clear intentions for what you do and do not want, and what you will and will not tolerate. Decide and visualize what victory will look and feel like when you achieve it.

Gather your strength, focus your mind on your intention, and embody the primordial power of the earth. Override hesitation and banish any limiting beliefs about what you deserve. Then charge ahead and secure the victory that is yours to claim.

BE THE QUEEN.

13. CLAIM THE THRONE

RULE, ABSOLUTELY, OVER YOUR DOMAIN, YOUR AFFAIRS, AND YOUR WORLD. KNOW, DEEP IN YOUR HEART THAT YOU ARE THE ULTIMATE AUTHORITY OVER YOUR LIFE AND LIFE CONDITIONS. ONCE YOU BELIEVE THIS WITH EVERY ATOM OF YOUR BEING, EVERYONE ELSE WILL TOO.

Don't quarrel, dissemble, or desperately seek to convince. Simply choose what you want and make it so. Also choose what you don't want, and dismiss it utterly.

Let this vampire faerie queen's confident self-possession be your own. Adopt her disdain for self-consciousness and self-apology. Open your body up to it. Try it on and steal it. Let it sink into your energy field and heart.

Be clear about your standards, and demand that those standards be unquestionably met. Don't suffer fools, and fools will dare not enter your sphere. Know, beyond all doubt and without the slightest self-consciousness, that whatever you desire, you are entitled to have.

This may be a message about seeking out, or stepping fully into, a role as a leader in a career, organization, or creative endeavor. Or it may simply be a message about owning the absolute authority that is inherent to who you are.

Of course, you must not shun all collaborations, conversations, and negotiations. Be an egalitarian ruler, not a tyrant. It is wise to seek counsel when you will benefit from others' help. And, just as you are the monarch of your life, others are the monarchs of theirs. So consider all perspectives and be empathetic and compassionate in good measure.

But always remember that when it comes to your life and circle of influence, no one controls you or rules over you. So concisely state your decree, wield your power, and expect the respect you deserve.

THIS IS AN INITIATION INTO A NEW LEVEL OF POWER.

14. INITIATION

GO BEYOND FEAR. GRADUATE TO GREATER MASTERY. BE WILLING TO FACE WHATEVER HAPPENS.

Courage is not repeatedly assuring yourself that everything will turn out okay. Courage is being open to, and willing to face, whatever happens.

At this threshold of power, we the vampire fae invite you to be a wise warrior priestess. But you are free to ignore this invitation. You can continue to hesitate and worry, feeling buffeted about by the whims of the absolute, believing that conditions must be a certain way for you to feel safe or okay. That is your right.

But if you do choose to be initiated, you must find your infinite nature within. You must identify and embody the part of you that abides in perfect equanimity, regardless of how things unfold.

The paradox is that when you set down your need for externally assured safety, you become truly safe. When you surrender your need to control the details, you will be free to wield your magic and live an uncommon life.

Full presence requires full acceptance of what is, what was, and what will be. It is only from this place of full ownership that you get to attract your desires and shape conditions according to your will.

The paradoxical nature of this message contains a veiled truth. You are both divine and human: infinite and temporary. Both conditions are simultaneously true. Where the human aspect is fearful and weak, the divine aspect is infinite and vast. The master in you knows there is nothing to fear because, amidst everything, your infinite nature remains. You can align one aspect with the other only when your human self willingly surrenders to the mystical and mysterious nature of the wild divine.

Go beyond your fear and summon your courage. Breathe, connect with your true nature by owning the past, accepting the present, and being willing to experience whatever may arise in the future. This is how you will claim your initiation and embody your mastery.

NOURISH YOURSELF.

15. FEED THE SPIRIT

Honor your soul's craving. Express your true nature. Pursue and savor that which fascinates, inspires, and satisfies.

Chase, overtake, and drink deeply of the lifeforce. Be satiated and sustained.

We predators are driven to hunt so we can satisfy our nutritional, spiritual, and psychological needs. We the vampire fae, much like other carnivorous species such as lions, owls, and sharks, feel most alive when we are stalking our next meal, and most relaxed after we have feasted on the lifeforce of our prey. This is not a character flaw, but an instinct we were born with — something we must do.

You, of course, need not hunt, kill, or feast on flesh. But you do need to follow the scent of your passion, amply nourish your body, and get lost in the pursuit of that which feeds your soul.

Just as we the vampire fae possess an intrinsic drive to catch and devour abusive and deceitful humans, you possess an intrinsic drive that is unique to you. You may feel most awake and alive, for example, when you are playing a sport, practicing a craft or artistic discipline, or making wise and incisive moves in your chosen career.

Provided you remain in integrity and affect no needless harm, the form your masterful expression takes is not as important as your commitment to it, and the sublime loss of self you experience while you are practicing it.

Allowing lifeforce energy to flow through you in such a way is certainly a need. When you ignore your soul's craving for prolonged focus on a cherished and well-chosen objective, you will suffer. The livewire of Divine Feminine energy will have no outlet, and you will feel toxic, restless, and uneasy.

This may also be a message to stop restricting food or otherwise neglecting your nutritional needs. We have observed that all humans must eat plenty of food, every day, multiple times per day, despite what some sources erroneously claim.

Put an end to your spiritual languishing and gnawing inner hunger. Allow your creativity and ambition to be channeled into a well-chosen outlet. Feast on abundant nourishment for your body, mind, and soul.

DRINK DEEPLY OF MOONLIGHT.

16. MOONLIGHT ELIXIR

Relax and receive. Quiet your insistent inner voice. Be still and allow blessings to come to you.

The cool light of the moon comes not from even a single spark of fire within, but from her legendary ability to soak up and reflect the radiant light of the sun.

For now, be like the moon. Set down your intensity, focus, worry, or drive to succeed. Stay where you are, relax deeply, and receive.

Your relationship with time and your schedule will naturally fluctuate. At times, you may get carried away with the belief that you must constantly be doing, acting, and making things happen. But just as the bustling day always fades away into the restorative night, you must balance your action with non-action and your sharpness with softness.

Take care of yourself. Meditate. Rest. Sleep. Spend time in a natural setting, go on a weekend getaway, or carve out some quiet alone time at home, as soon as your schedule permits.

If your thoughts are like a raging storm, don't fight against the storm or judge yourself for overthinking. Just notice the clear, silent openness around and underneath your thoughts as often as you can. Identify not with the thoughts, but with the silence. The silence is the sky of who you are. The thoughts are just the weather patterns passing through. As you consciously relax your body and mind, do your best to slow the raging hurricane of your inner monologue down to a light drizzle. In time, the clouds of excess thought will part and allow you to bathe in the cool and rejuvenating light of the moon.

When you set down the burden of your thoughts and responsibilities, new avenues of magic will naturally flow to you. Relaxation of body and mind will open channels of possibility and power.

Imbibe the moonlight elixir and receive the harmonizing nourishment you need.

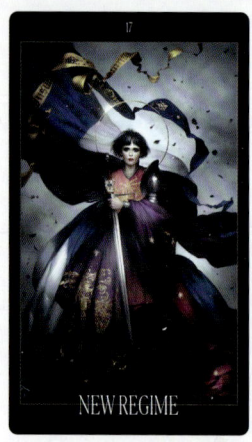

17. NEW REGIME

SEE YOURSELF IN A NEW AND MORE GLORIOUS LIGHT. RELEASE SELF-CRITICISM. CLAIM THE POWER THAT IS YOURS TO WIELD.

In the light of your fierce inner clarity, the old regime cannot stand.

The old regime, in this instance, may be a literal person or group who seems to hold power over you. Or it could consist of past patterns of worry or self-doubt that have been holding you back and keeping you small.

Perhaps someone told you that you were a sinner and you believed them, so you gave up your intrinsic morals and moral compass to a spiritual creed, leader, or institution. You might have picked up the idea that it was wrong for you to enjoy luxury or to draw attention to yourself through your beauty, uniqueness,

OVERTHROW THE DICTATORSHIP OF LIES.

or talent. It could be that you inadvertently internalized beliefs about your sexuality or gender as being inherently deviant, shameful, or weak. Or someone may seem to be oppressing you by perpetuating an illusion of authority.

Whatever lies you have been believing, see through them and triumph over them now. Do not suffer under their weight for a single moment more.

The story that is holding you back may not be specific. It may maintain, for example, that you're just plain wrong and bad, and if you don't know why, that's just more proof that you don't measure up or don't deserve.

But there's a new queen in town. You. See yourself filled with the light of divine right and personal authority. In this newly discovered, newly claimed role, you glow. You are breathtaking — a gorgeous and regal sight to behold.

While you examine the concepts, dynamics, and paradigms to rewrite and transcend, be aware that these patterns of toxic inner or outer domination may not have originated with you, but rather with your caregivers, ancestors, or culture. But no matter where they came from, hanging onto them is holding you back, and you haven't the slightest obligation to do so.

Vanquish the old regime and transcend to a new level of truth. Rewrite your story so it's in alignment with your intrinsic power. And be the queen.

THE EARTH PROVIDES.

18. RICHES OF GAIA

Tap into the rich flow of abundance from the earth. A wealth of luxury surrounds you now. Allow blessings to flow to you endlessly, and be rich.

We the *baobhan sith* are always rich, because affluence and physical resources flow to us endlessly. We will now share with you a simple but vital practice that will help you unlock the same degree of abundance and luck.

First, go to a serene natural setting where you can be alone, or find a calming indoor space with a comfortable place to sit or recline. Settle in and take some time to relax your whole body. Bring to mind the fertile, nourishing quality of the verdant earth. Consider the blessings of our sacred planet, such as lush greenery, sparkling water, delicious scents, and nourishing foods. Marvel at these blessings and see if you can feel a natural sense of gratitude well up from within. This will create a vibrational shift that will open you up to blessings and wealth.

Also, today and in the days ahead, engage with presence in grounding and sensualizing behaviors, such as standing barefoot on the earth, walking in nature, gardening, cooking, eating, dancing, stretching, taking a warm bath, or mindfully inhaling natural botanical scents.

While there's nothing wrong with thinking, planning, and problem solving, this is a nudge to stop living solely in your head. Let your awareness fill your entire body and aura. Also expand outward — sense that even your body is but one small part of the consciousness of the planet. When you do so, the opulence of the earth will become available to you. You will unlock the riches of Gaia, which will begin to ceaselessly and generously flow.

While you will, of course, work within the realm of form to make and execute plans to help your financial increase along, be sure to begin with the essential inner shift outlined for you here.

Inhabit your body and feel your oneness with nature. Relish all the beauty that already exists for you, within and around you. Listen deeply, relax fully, act when you feel guided, and allow yourself to receive the luxurious riches of the earth.

19. DIVINE IDENTITY

YOU ARE IMMORTAL.

YOU ARE BOTH HUMAN AND DIVINE. KNOW YOURSELF AS BOTH. THIS WILL ELEVATE AND TRANSFORM YOUR EXPERIENCE.

Like the *baobhan sith*, you are a wild creature of great power — both mortal and immortal at once.

Your existence is a paradox. On the one hand, you are temporary, limited, and fallible. And at the very same time, you are eternal, infinite, and vast. You are at once both acorn and forest, ocean and raindrop.

When you identify solely with your temporary human self, you feel weaker and less effective than you actually are. But if you were to identify solely as an immortal creature, you would be delusional. Your relationships would suffer, and you would become out of sync with the everyday rhythm of your humanness.

That's why you must hold both truths within you simultaneously, even though they appear to be at odds. And you must not believe that one truth diminishes the other. Neither is partially true. Both are absolute. You are utterly human, and you are entirely divine.

Nor should it lessen your identification as a divine being to know that all humans are equally divine, for in your shared divinity, you and they are one. Your human ego may mistakenly seek to claim divine identity as yours alone, but this is a misunderstanding; for the Divine Consciousness is not a form of specialness, but rather an affirmation of the interconnected oneness of all.

When you believe in and draw upon your divinity, you become empowered to heal yourself and others, and to harmonize your internal and external worlds with the infinite light and mellifluous resonance of the cosmos.

Close your eyes, relax, and breathe deeply. Call upon and channel the infinite power of the earth and cosmos. Sense this power within you, reminding you of your infinite nature. Know, deeply, your true, divinely aligned desires and will. Then use your transcendent authority to manifest positive change.

FACE THE TRUTH.

20. DESPERATE FOR DECEPTION

YOU ARE WILFULLY CONCEALING AN IMPORTANT TRUTH OR FABRICATING YOUR REALITY IN A DESPERATE BID TO FEEL MORE POWERFUL OR SECURE. ADMIT THE LIE. BEING HONEST WILL HELP YOU SUCCEED AND FIND PEACE.

Your own dishonesty is perpetuating the hassles and complexities that appear to plague you. Discover the self-deception under which you are currently operating, or come clean about the lie you are telling to others to establish greater ease.

It's time for some earnest self-reflection. Look at the stories you are telling yourself and others about your present situation. Do you believe you need to accomplish something to prove your worth to yourself or others? Is there a cultural, organizational, or family expectation you are seeking to fulfill that doesn't feel authentic to you? Have you been putting your faith in someone who is not trustworthy, or unwittingly handing your authority over to a person, group, or situation? Or are you deliberately deceiving someone else?

Humans are a socially and psychologically complex species, and there will be times in every human life during which deception holds sway. No one is immune from falling under the hypnotic spell of a beautiful lie, false messiah, or unworthy cause. So there's no reason to feel ashamed.

If you have been operating under or instigating a powerful deception for a prolonged length of time, there can be an added challenge in adjusting your outlook. No one wants to discover they have been devoting their time, energy, or emotions to something that was never valid or real. However, the longer you operate under this inaccuracy, the more time and energy you will waste.

Place a hand on your heart. Take a breath. Assert to yourself and the universe that you are willing to expose the deception. Then see the truth, admit it, and make things right.

GET SOME SPACE.

21. YOUR OWN WORLD

Your soul requires free and unscheduled alone time to dream, imagine, and contemplate. Cancel plans if you need to or just carve out some time to relax, recharge, play, and get back in touch with yourself.

Just as the *baobhan sith* require extended periods of solitude, your wild spirit needs regular intervals of seclusion and silence, where you can be yourself and live, for a time, in a world all your own. Providing yourself with this basic spiritual necessity will bring about the inner shift that will align you with the answer or outcome you seek.

Is there somewhere you can go when you want to be alone?

Do you have a room, or a corner of a room, or even a closet where you can set up an altar, meditate, pray, and write in your journal? If you live in a lively and well-populated home, would it be possible for you to wake up before everyone else, or stay up for a short while after everybody has gone to bed? For the sake of your creativity, spirituality, and joy, it's vital for you to have time and space where you can plan, formulate, and daydream without interruption.

What's more, it's often a good idea for you to retreat for a day or more, and take a break from other people and your phone. If possible, this retreat can take place in your own home, but you may need to schedule some time away. Consider reserving a rental property or campsite, or you might offer to house-sit for a friend.

If any of the above suggestions seem completely beyond your reach, look deeply at why this is so, and take steps to change whatever seems to be preventing you from getting the time and space that your spirit so desperately requires.

There are some wild creatures—like us and like yourself—who will suffer if they do not get to linger in the twilight and silence, alone.

22. MAKE A WISH

A PORTAL OF POSSIBILITY IS OPEN TO YOU NOW. DECIDE WHAT YOU WANT, THEN CLAIM IT. FIRST ASK FOR IT, THEN BELIEVE, AND TRUST THAT YOU SHALL RECEIVE.

In this moment, there is something specific for which your heart of hearts dearly yearns. What is it? Acknowledge it, then wish for it.

You are always imbued with the divine power to create positive change according to your will, and to bring about the conditions you desire. But there are certain times when this truth is especially available to you: times when you are poised to step up into a new level of expansion, beauty, and divine magnetism, near instantaneously. This is one of those times.

WHAT YOU WANT, YOU SHALL HAVE.

In the past, you may have felt limited by money, or opportunity, or destiny. Now is a time to leave such beliefs of lack and limitation behind. It will help to use the magical phrase, "What if." As in: "*What if* I could have exactly the life I envision? *What if* I could achieve the success I would most enjoy, and manifest the blessings and resources I would most like to have? *What if* there were no limits? *What if* the earth provides, and the universe really is on my side?"

Breathe, relax, and answer these questions, not just with your mind, but also with your body and spirit. How would it feel for these positive affirmations to be absolutely, abidingly true? This is the magical act of expanding what is possible, of entering this portal of granted wishes and realized dreams.

Make a wish. State your intentions. Imagine, feel, and trust they are already so, and be grateful. Allow the conscious, creative light of the cosmos to flow into your energy field. We predict that you will easily and naturally manifest all that you desire, and more.

SEE DEEPLY INTO THE HEART OF THINGS.

23. SEE BEYOND

CULTIVATE YOUR SPIRITUAL GIFTS. YOUR PSYCHIC AND INTUITIVE POWERS ARE STRONG AND CLEAR. CLAIM THEM AND MAKE USE OF THEM NOW.

You, like the vampire fae, are highly intuitive. Be willing to see, trust, and know. Connect with the spirits. Gaze at the truth from all angles. Channel your considerable spiritual power toward the seeking and finding of your desire.

Employ your psychic gifts, not just now, but always. Open your third eye and see, sense, or know what the invisible realm is communicating to you.

This may be a message to consult your intuition for a specific purpose, or to employ it in your life's work or as part of your spiritual practice and path.

First, though, set the intention to protect and bolster your heart. Also visualize bright light surrounding you in a cocoon, keeping overwhelm and negativity of all varieties at bay.

Using your spiritual gifts opens you up to the subtle realm. This requires some shielding, for if you are open to everything—all emotions, thoughts, energies, and spirits—you will not only feel uncomfortable, but you will also find it difficult to receive useful information or to discern what you most need to know.

The red rose in this image reminds you to begin with, and to be guided, always, by the fierce strength of your courageous heart. Draw upon your passion. Be energized and motivated by the power of love.

This vampire fae's amethyst headpiece is both a receptor of divine wisdom and a protective amulet that shields her from all that is not for her highest good. Similarly, gaze bravely beyond the realm of form, but first consciously attune to the stream of wisdom that flows directly from the ether to you.

Call on the infinite light of the cosmos to nourish you, connect with the core of the earth to ground you, and invoke bright light to surround and protect you. This way, you need never fear as you employ your gifts of clairvoyance, clairaudience, claircognizance, and clairsentience, as well as your mediumship abilities to communicate with spirits and see beyond the veil.

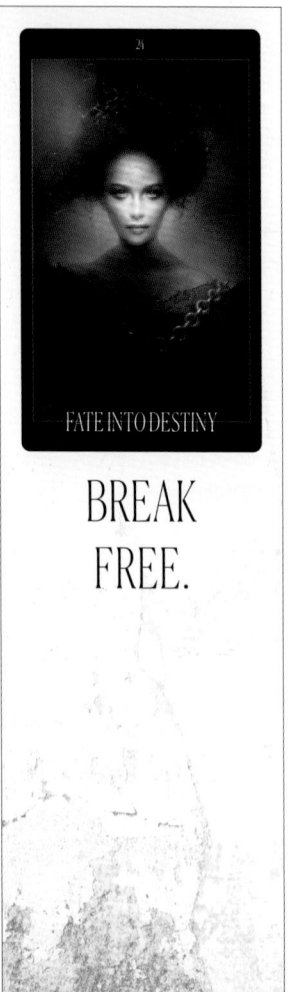

BREAK FREE.

24. FATE INTO DESTINY

LIBERATE YOURSELF FROM THE CHAINS OF FATE. TRANSFORM AN UNLUCKY BREAK INTO AN EXPANSIVE DESTINY. RECOGNIZE THE PATTERN AND UNCOVER THE LESSON IT CONTAINS SO YOU CAN RISE UP AND OUT OF THIS CHALLENGE FOR GOOD.

You are bumping up against an ancestral or past-life challenge. The origin of this pattern may be hundreds or even thousands of years old. Even if you don't consciously remember how or when it started, we are asking you to look at it again, so you can heal, evolve, and finally move on.

Don't use this as an opportunity to punish or berate yourself. It's an error to imagine that an ancestral or past-life challenge is your fault. Instead, see this as something you have volunteered to heal in this lifetime — not just for yourself, but also on behalf of your family, community, and culture.

If you're not sure what pattern this card is pointing to, ask yourself: "What's familiar here? How has this shown up for me (or my family) before in a similar form?" Also tune in to your intuition. What feels ancient and fated about this situation? What feels like something that you've seen before, that may even have roots in the distant past?

Once you know what old cycle is showing up to be healed, close your eyes. Relax your body as you breathe for a bit. Then ask us to show you how to learn the lesson, break the chains, and free yourself from this timeworn labyrinth or trap. You will receive our guidance as a clear inner knowing, or perhaps a picture in your awareness or a word or phrase that arises in your mind.

You can't go around this issue. You can only go through it. So be brave. Step fully into the heart of this challenge, and let us show you a new way of seeing, processing, or dealing with it. It's time to break the cycle so you can finally be free.

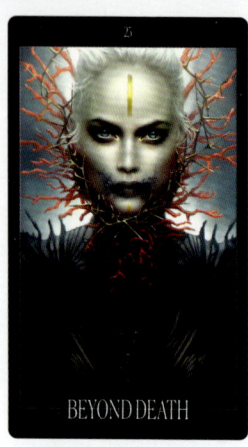

DESCEND, WITHOUT FEAR, INTO THE UNDERWORLD.

25. BEYOND DEATH

UNLOCK LIFE BY TRANSCENDING THE FEAR OF DEATH. BE COURAGEOUS. LET NOTHING LIMIT YOU OR HOLD YOU BACK.

We the vampire fae recognize certain goddesses as our kith and kin, for they visited the darkest night and traversed the furthest circle of death to find their power.

The goddess Inanna assured her authority over all other divinities when she descended into the underworld and then found her way out, emerging back into light and life, not only unscathed, but also brighter and stronger than before.

Hecate, goddess of spirits and necromancy, holds the key to the afterlife, where all wisdom everlastingly dwells.

Kali is the goddess of both death and ultimate, all-conquering power.

Similarly, in our triumph over mortality, we reign over all mysteries and have access to the secret knowledge of the ages.

When you cease to hand your power over to death—when you willingly, bravely go beyond the limiting and obsessive illusion that death is the actual end—nothing can stop you. It is only there, beyond death, where you will finally claim your authority and find your groove.

Of course, while you are in human form, you will have the instinct of self-preservation, and we would like for you to keep that. Healthy fear is vital to well-being. It reminds you to take the practical precautions that keep you safe. So this is certainly not a message about behaving recklessly, putting yourself in harm's way, or in any way hastening your human body's demise. In fact, when you see yourself as infinite, you will find so much freedom and enjoyment in the human experience, you will have a natural desire to revel in it and make it last.

If you knew, beyond all doubt, that your true self was indestructible, and inextricably interwoven with the fabric of everything, what would you do? How would you approach your life, your relationships, and your current situation? What revolutionary ideas and bold actions would that perspective inspire?

Beyond the fear of death, there is bright fierceness. See beyond the petty fears that have previously held you back and diminished your freedom. Know yourself as eternal, and unlock all wisdom.

26. AKASHIC UNWEAVING

RENOUNCE AND DISMANTLE AN OLD AGREEMENT OR VOW. IN A PAST LIFE OR ERA, YOU MADE AN INNER OR OUTER PRONOUNCEMENT, WHICH THEN WOVE ITSELF INTO THE TAPESTRY OF YOUR FATE. NOW YOU MUST UNWEAVE.

UNMAKE WHAT HAS BEEN MADE.

Untie the knots and unravel the threads of the story.

It's possible that at some point in the distant or recent past, you made a conscious and deliberate vow, such as a commitment to a partnership or a cause. Or it could have been something subtler and less overt, such as an unhealthy relationship dynamic you bought into, a choice you made to shield your heart, or a silent promise to never let yourself hope for a cherished goal.

You already know what this card is asking you to release. If you think you don't know, close your eyes, relax, and take some deep breaths. Ask us for clarity. Open your consciousness and allow us to show you. You see? The answer is there.

Even if this narrative's origins are in a past life, you can sense its quality and contents by examining your experiences in this life.

Look at this pattern with compassion and from a number of angles. Your pain and confusion were difficult to bear, and you did your best to formulate an approach and construct a paradigm that would guard you and help you get through. Place a loving hand on your heart and another on your belly. Breathe, understand, and unclench.

Now, let go. If you ask, we will clear away and delete this old pattern from your energy field in all directions and dimensions of time and space. As we do so, allow your dreaming mind to shift, your memories to be reframed, and your subconscious and conscious minds to transform.

Imagine this old pattern like a heavy cloud in the dark night. With our help, it is breaking up, dissolving, unraveling, and blowing away. Awaken now to the shining jewel of the waxing crescent moon, lighting up the sky — a bright new beginning and cycle of time.

27. AMBASSADOR

FIND COMMON GROUND. BUILD A BRIDGE OF COMMUNICATION. SHARE YOUR PERSPECTIVES AND LISTEN DEEPLY AS OTHERS SHARE THEIR PERSPECTIVES WITH YOU.

It's natural to fear the unfamiliar. But when you make the choice to get acquainted with people of other cultures, demographics, religions, and ideologies, magic happens. You expand your consciousness and sphere of influence, you make new friends and allies, and you feel safer and more at home in the world.

We the vampire fae are accustomed to being misunderstood. For centuries, humans have distrusted us, tried to avoid us, and made us the subjects of gruesome tales. And

TRANSCEND YOUR DIFFERENCES AND CONNECT.

yet here we are anyway, sharing our wisdom to help you prevail.

Similarly, override your own suspicion or the suspicion of others by approaching a person or group with curiosity and goodwill. Even if it feels uncomfortable at first, persist. Be steadfast, courageous, and determined, but also be patient and respectful. Don't push. Let it take as long as it takes.

Your role as ambassador is a prestigious responsibility. First, make sure you are not subjecting yourself to physical abuse or verbal attack, for these are conditions that bar the way forward into unity, fairness, and egalitarian relations. Once you've paved the way for true connection, transcend your ego's constant desire to be right. Then, inwardly lift your awareness up and out of the conflict. From this elevated perspective, proceed.

This may also be a message that recovering or establishing a sense of comfortable familiarity may take some time, but it is not out of reach. Beginning a new job, starting a new relationship, or moving to a new city are all moments when time and fortitude are required before you begin to feel at home.

Our differences have the potential to teach us and make us stronger. But first, you must tap into your most impeccable wisdom and lay the groundwork for mutual respect.

JOY RETURNS.

28. MIDWINTER

BUTTERFLIES BRING HOPE IN THE MIDDLE OF WINTER. EVEN AFTER HEARTBREAK AND STRUGGLE, YOUR MOOD WILL LIFT. MAGIC SPARKLES AMIDST THE GLOOM.

In the darkest heart of winter, miraculous butterflies appear.

You may be weary and despairing. You may feel hollow, hopeless, and bereft of joy.

At midwinter, while it is still frozen and cold, there are glimmers of beauty to be found. While it may still be months before the snow melts, you can find the radiant magic within the romantic melancholy of the ice.

Looking back at difficult times, you find great value in the songs that brought you comfort, the friends who understood your feelings, and the moments of laughter amidst the pain. This time is the same. Revel in the unique feel of your current situation.

It's also true that profound struggles carry profound wisdom. Without them, you would be far less empathetic and wise. And you would never know just how resilient and courageous you are.

The precious and mystical quality of this time in your life may be subtle, but it's most certainly there. Enter the present moment, and you will find it hiding in the scent of incense, the taste of hot coffee, and the sound of a crackling flame.

Life is a full-spectrum experience: Every season contains heartache and happiness, pleasure and pain. In each moment, there are various waves of energy and emotion in play. Be open to everything. Be kind to yourself through it all, and expect a positive outcome, even if you can't imagine what it will be. Be curious about how your challenges will ultimately work out for the best.

This may not be an easy time, but it is a precious one. Like a butterfly, you will soon emerge from it with wings — in a brand new, glorious form.

29. NOT A SINNER

INTERNALIZED BELIEFS ABOUT UNWORTHINESS HAVE GOT TO GO. RECOGNIZE AND BANISH TOXIC PROGRAMMING. CAST OFF THE YOKE OF EMBARRASSMENT.

STOP FEELING ASHAMED.

We the vampire fae were present when the false messages of "sin" and "sinfulness" first cast their ugly pall over your culture. We witnessed these messages twisting and subverting simple pleasures, further disenfranchising the already disenfranchised, and siphoning away your joy and delight.

In fact, it was right around this time that we chose to intervene. After all, we punish those who would otherwise go unpunished: the men who betrayed or abused their mortal wives, daughters, and sisters. The less power we perceived you to possess, the more we attempted to right such grievous wrongs.

We want you to see that you are holding a false belief that you are fundamentally incomplete and flawed. It is possible someone is underscoring this message to keep you in their thrall. A partner may be undermining your self-worth. An authority figure may be manipulating you. A spiritual group may be insisting you need them for the sake of your soul.

You may be operating under an internalized, disempowering paradigm that you learned from your family or culture. Examine your consciousness. Look deeply at any explicit teachings or implicit assumptions that actively diminish and call into question your intrinsic worth.

You are entitled to freedom and you deserve to flourish. Even if you believe you have made a legitimate mistake, be kind, forgiving, and compassionate with yourself. Everyone struggles. Everyone blunders. Everyone is learning as they go.

Detect and reject old stories that cast you in the light of shame. Gather up your dignity, refuse to accept cultish programming or toxic relationship dynamics, and know that you are entitled to thrive.

PROTECTIVE VEIL

SHORE UP YOUR POWER.

30. PROTECTIVE VEIL

REFUSE TO BE DEPLETED. GUARD YOUR LIGHT. WORK YOUR MAGIC TO SURROUND YOURSELF IN A PROTECTIVE VEIL.

It's possible that you are currently exhausted or pushed to your limit. Others may be attempting to take advantage of you, prey on you, or siphon off your light. Or, you may have temporarily forgotten your right to set boundaries around your energy, attention, and time.

At this very moment, take a deep breath and ask us to shield and watch over you. See or sense us surrounding your head with a silver circlet and draping a bay laurel over your head and around your shoulders. Also sense us draping this ethereal herb over the front of your body to bolster your heart and safeguard your aura.

Spiritual immunity and physical immunity are often linked: Your body's wellness and your spirit's wellness each mirror and support the other. So this may be a message to rest and recharge. Eat healthy food, drink nourishing herbal tea (such as nettle, red clover, or red raspberry leaf), and get plenty of sleep.

How and with whom have you been spending your time and energy? Are there any imbalances you can remedy? For example, you may be involved in responsibilities or relationships that no longer serve you, or in which you are not comfortable being yourself or speaking your truth. Also notice how your attention may be stolen by modern distractions, and how you may be systematically harmed by deliberate deception perpetuated by those who benefit from your lack of self-worth.

As you breathe and allow us to protect, recalibrate, and recharge you, ask yourself if there are any relationships, projects, goals, or self-care habits you would like to make more time for. Ignoring your needs will not fail to diminish your energy, health, and overall enjoyment of life.

Step back from what you don't want, make time for what you do want, and take your power back. Shield and protect your personal energy now.

31. FRESH AIR

CLEAR THE ENERGY IN YOUR ENVIRONMENT. BOLSTER AND REFRESH YOUR AURA. LIFT YOUR SPIRITS, PAY ATTENTION TO BEAUTY, AND ENJOY YOUR LIFE.

Even the fiercest faeries must lighten up sometimes. Fine-tune your energy, spruce up your environment, and lovingly adorn and beautify your body to shift your energy for the better. These practices are not luxuries reserved for those days when you happen to have extra time on your hands, but vital imperatives. Prioritize them and you will boost your outlook and rediscover your joy.

Clear clutter from your environment. Let go of everything that you don't love, use, or need. Then create more buoyancy in your space with things like wind dancers, light catchers, and prayer

LET A FRESH BREEZE BLOW THROUGH.

flags. Consider redecorating with lighter fabrics and colors as well.

As soon as you have a little time, open your closet and dresser and pull out all your clothes and accessories. Consider each item individually before putting it back. Does it fit you perfectly? When you wear it, do you feel beautiful, powerful, and free? If not, pack it up and make plans to give it away. Then consider: What clothes or accessories will help you radiate everyday magic? Even your pajamas can help you celebrate and enjoy your sensual human existence. You're getting dressed anyway, so let your clothes be wings that help you gracefully flutter like a monarch through the garden of your life experience.

Tend also to your personal energy field. Schedule an energy healing, or cleanse and fine-tune your own energy. Take a sea-salt or Epsom-salt bath, perform a chakra-clearing meditation, purify yourself with sound (such as a chime, bell, or chant), or bathe yourself in smoke from a sustainably sourced sage bundle or another cleansing herb.

Cultivate lightness within and without to amplify beauty and magnetize the blessings you desire.

UNLEASH YOUR SPLENDOR.

32. ENTITLED TO SHINE

SHINE YOUR LIGHT. SHARE YOUR GIFTS. BE SEEN.

Like a peacock, let your aura be a glorious fan of pride and prestige.

Do not hide your essence away. There is nothing virtuous about blending in and concealing your unique brilliance and beauty from the world. Aren't you bored of being shy? Isn't it getting old to constantly be worried that you will be rejected or unwelcome, instead of knowing, absolutely, that you are entitled to shine?

Being seen for who you are feels vulnerable, but you can handle it. Be who you are, share who you are, and claim the divine role that only you can.

Don't worry about what's in or out of style. How you show up in the world is not contingent on what other people are doing or saying. So tune into what's true for you. What truth do you want to speak? What actions do you want to take? What shame can you let go of, and what old secret are you finally ready to share? You're the queen — your own rules are the only ones you need to follow. Radiate your uniqueness and take joy in your self-determination.

As you get clear on who you are and align your inner and outer selves, you may realize you want to switch something up, such as where you live, what music you listen to, or the style of clothes you wear. This is not a coincidence. When you attune to, and embody, your true essence, you will readjust on multiple levels. Get excited about these inner nudges. Revel in them — they are affirmations of self-respect. Let them magnify your resonance and supercharge your power.

It is not noble to consistently lie low, hang back, and stifle your fabulous charm. Share what you want to share. Let your light be a beacon that attracts and inspires others. You offer a gift to the world simply by being you.

DARK JEWEL

YOU ARE A WAYSHOWER.

33. DARK JEWEL

WALKING THROUGH DARKNESS HAS MADE YOU FIERCE. USE YOUR WISDOM TO NAVIGATE THROUGH THE SHADOWS . ACCESS THE MAGIC IN YOUR MYSTERIOUS DEPTHS.

Your past suffering has blessed you with immense wisdom and stamina. Use this mastery to navigate a present challenge or to help someone else find their way through.

Embrace, also, your more eternal and nuanced charm. Innocence is sweet, and youth has its fleeting shine, but making it through struggle and heartache has imbued you with a mesmerizing dimension that has only increased with each unflinching gaze into the velvet dark.

If your vibe tends toward the gothic and macabre, honor your offbeat aesthetic flavor. If you are cynical or comically dark, celebrate the sense of humor that you have adopted to survive.

But if you have been denying or concealing your less cheery and more hidden aspects, begin now to embody the full spectrum of who you are, all the way down to the subterranean dregs of your soul. Claim all of it. Own all of it. For there in your depths is where your power lies. And that power is formidable. Indeed, you are more than equal to what you currently face. Your deepest darkness is your glorious strength.

Where others might get squeamish, get brave. When others may run away, rush forward. You have painstakingly earned this power you now possess. Wield it now, and you will not only succeed — you will also emerge even stronger, wiser, and more glorious than you were before.

You are not a transparent, breakable piece of glass, but a coal-black, diamond-hard jewel. Intense pressure has bestowed immaculate resilience. Use this resilience to help yourself. Or this may be a message to share your hard-earned gifts, perhaps through a discipline, modality, or art

Look within and you will discover you already know what to do. Fear nothing and move through the darkness with grace.

34. LADY IN WHITE

IT'S TIME TO HEAL AND MOVE ON. BE ATTENTIVE TO YOUR OWN NEEDS. ALLOW US TO HELP YOU REGAIN YOUR WHOLENESS AND REESTABLISH YOUR INDEPENDENCE.

HURT NOW, BUT NOT FOREVER.

For centuries, and in many parts of the world, people have glimpsed wraithlike female figures floating through the night, dressed all in white. They are not *baobhan sith*, but rather what we seek to prevent: ghosts of human women whose hopes and dreams were shattered by heartbreak and grief.

Even if it seems like your heart has been broken into a million pieces and the light of your joy has been smothered under the ice of the coldest night, you can reassemble your heart and rekindle your fire. Your fighting spirit is recoverable, and it is far closer and more accessible than you know.

Even if you have been a victim, you need see yourself in this role no longer. You are always entitled to your well-being. After a trauma or tragedy, when you feel your feelings, you can then let them go. Let not your pain be your identity. You must not expect to be damaged for all time.

Place a hand on your heart. Breathe into your heartache and send yourself support. Remember that every mortal being suffers, and gain comfort from knowing you are not alone. But also remember that your suffering shall pass, and is indeed dwindling even now. Invoke our help, and allow us to bolster your spirit, soothe your sadness, and restore your power and your joy.

Pay attention to what will nourish you and replenish your spirit in the way that will be most beneficial. Rest if you need to rest. It's also a good idea to laugh, play, create, spend time with friends, and engage in other everyday therapeutic activities.

While your heart may ache at times as the result of a past wound, it is amazing in its ability to regenerate and return to a state of thriving. As you incrementally regain your strength and refresh your outlook, notice and celebrate the blessings that are here for you all along the way.

35. THE MORRIGAN

ASK FOR AND RECEIVE STRATEGIC GUIDANCE. YOU ARE FACING SOME VARIETY OF POWER NEGOTIATION OR PERSONAL TRIAL. YOU WILL PREVAIL IF YOU LISTEN CLOSELY, AND CAREFULLY FOLLOW THE MORRIGAN'S COUNSEL.

KNOW YOUR ENEMY.

The Morrigan, whose name means "queen of nightmares" or "phantom queen," is the great Celtic goddess of birth, death, war, destruction, fertility, and sex. She is a shapeshifter and can take the form of any animal or human she chooses. A queen among vampire fae, the Morrigan is here to whisper battle secrets in your ear.

First, know your enemy. Who or what are you currently facing on the battlefield of life? It may be a person, a group, a situation, an idea, or something within yourself that you must face. If you're not sure, relax, close your eyes, and ask the Morrigan to show you the answer.

Second, know yourself. What has held you back before in similar situations? What do you care about, what do you fear, what do you have to lose, and what do you have to gain by facing this challenge? If you are willing to be honest with yourself, the Morrigan will illuminate what you need to know.

Once you are clear on the battle and the stakes, get clear about your intentions for how you want things to unfold. What will victory look like for you? What is your ideal outcome? How will you feel when you experience it? Attune to the frequency of this outcome by feeling as if it is already so.

You may be surprised by what you intuitively hear, sense, see, or know. The Morrigan may offer visions or information that are unexpected or seemingly unrelated to the topic at hand. You will know the direction comes from her if it feels both fair and uncompromising. The Morrigan will guide you to be swift and perceptive, fierce but just.

Rest assured, the Morrigan's shrewd and incisive guidance is here for you. Ask, relax, breathe, and gain the insights you need.

ANCESTOR MAGIC

36. ANCESTOR MAGIC

YOU ARE NOT ALONE. GATHER WISDOM FROM THOSE WHO HAVE COME BEFORE. COUNTLESS FEMALE ANCESTORS ARE READY TO LEND YOU THEIR MAGIC AND HELP YOU SUCCEED.

ASK THE GRAND-MOTHERS.

You are connected to everything, in all directions of time. You are an acorn on a branch in a long-established grove of thriving oaks. The roots on these trees go deep, and you contain both ancient and future forests within your spiritual DNA. You stretch endlessly into the past and future, as far as the eye can see.

Draw upon all the illumination, wisdom, and resilience of this interconnection now. Call on the grandmothers—all the many witches and wise women that both contributed to your existence and dwell within your being—to support you, guide you, and give you strength.

All this power is already present within you. All the knowledge and understanding you need are accessible to you. Listen to your ancestors, activate your clear remembering, and claim your spiritual legacy now. Work your magic not as the acorn, but as the verdant and deep-rooted grove.

You may want to visit a cemetery where one or more of your female ancestors were buried. Offer flowers, a beloved beverage, or food and ask this foremother for her guidance and support.

Another way to connect with the grandmothers is to create an ancestor altar. Appropriate items for ancestor altars include photos of your foremothers, one or more of their past belongings, favorite edible or drinkable treats, or anything else that holds their essence or energy. Light a candle on the altar and consider adding additional offerings such as incense, flowers, or fruit.

Take the time and make the effort to connect with your feminine spiritual lineage and roots. Ask for help, wisdom, guidance, and support. And it will certainly be there for you.

37. VISIONARY

SEE THE BIG PICTURE AND GAZE INTO THE FUTURE. IT IS ALWAYS A CHALLENGE TO BE AHEAD OF YOUR TIME. BUT PERSEVERE, FOR YOUR PERSPECTIVE WILL USHER IN A SWEEPING POSITIVE CHANGE.

With hindsight, it's easier to see the visionaries who deserve to be lauded and praised. But in the moment, they are often underappreciated (or even punished or shunned) for their revolutionary perspectives and gifts.

Let us bolster your morale and fortify your resolve. Even if others do not share your vision or perceive the subtler layer and less-obvious factors at play, do not be dissuaded. Persist. Trust yourself and your insight. Follow through on your plans to innovate, pioneer, and create.

BRING YOUR INNER VISION INTO FORM.

You may perceive an injustice that no one else is talking about, or formulate a solution that hasn't previously been considered. Perhaps there is a style of creativity that appeals to you that isn't yet in fashion, or an unpopular option your heart of hearts desires to choose.

While this may be a message about your creative work or career path, it could also be related to your community, family, primary relationship, or other interpersonal concerns. For example, you may feel called to leave your hometown despite your family's protests, or to explore a spiritual path your partner doesn't understand.

Ask yourself: "If I were to release myself from tradition and stop feeling limited by the expectations of others, what would I do? If I were to honour my uniqueness and go my own way, what choice would I make?"

This moment requires courage. You must venture alone, into the mysterious unknown. But you will not feel lonely, odd, or invisible forever. Your bold action will make you a beacon, and others of like mind will be drawn to you. You will find your place in this world, and seen and unseen forces will conspire to help you bring your vision into form.

ENLIST THE FETCH

YOUR SOUL'S WILD ASPECT WILL HELP YOU.

38. ENLIST THE FETCH

ALLY WITH YOUR ANIMAL SPIRIT. WORK YOUR MAGIC AND CONSULT YOUR INTUITION. DRAW UPON THE PRIMORDIAL WISDOM YOU HAVE ALWAYS POSSESSED.

All humans with whom we vampire fae consort—that is, the witches and magical ones—have what is called a "fetch." This is an etheric familiar. It is an aspect of your very own spirit that takes animal form. While your fetch is a part of you, it is also a loving and beloved friend. You can enlist this creature to protect you, provide you with insight, and go places you can't physically go to perform reconnaissance or keep an eye out for potential threats.

Your fetch may be a snake (like the fetch in the image), but it may also be a parrot, a lion, an owl, a butterfly, a unicorn, an otter, or a vole. In fact, this companion and component of your soul may appear in any conceivable animal form.

Working with your fetch can help you call your power back when you have been robbed of it, or when a dysfunctional relationship dynamic has caused it to be undermined.

If you haven't yet familiarized yourself with your fetch, do so now. Make sure you have at least half an hour or so to yourself. Light a candle, close your eyes, breathe deeply, and ask this creature to appear to you on the inner plane. Incense and entrancing instrumental music are optional but helpful tools for opening your psychic channel.

Once you are relaxed and calm, ask yourself: "If I knew the animal form of my fetch, what would it be?" This answer is there for you. Trust what you receive. Once you see your fetch with your inner eye, ask what your fetch's name is. Allow yourself to know.

Then, express your love and appreciation, and ask for the specific support you require. Request protection, insight, help with a certain goal or intention, or simply cultivate a strong sense of supportive solidarity with your fetch and your inherent spiritual power.

Ask your fetch for the help you need, and you will receive it. You can draw upon this power now and always.

BASK IN YOUR OWN GLOW.

39. LIGHT THE NIGHT

Persist. Draw upon your spirit's radiance and make your own magic. Stay the course, despite any temporary discouragement or seeming setbacks.

You are not a summer butterfly, requiring a comfortable environment to thrive. You are hearty and wild, magnificent and deep. Inclement conditions need not dissuade you from your purpose. In fact, they can make you stronger and help you commit further to your path.

How do you want to live? What magic would you like to make? How would you like to feel? What gifts of positive change do you want to present to the world? Be fortified by the heroism this requires. Let nothing dishearten you — not your own challenges, the challenges of others, or collective injustices. Rather, let them stoke your resolve, contribute to your wisdom, and burnish the beauty you create.

If you are drawn to a career, calling, or artistic pursuit, commit to it. While your enthusiasm will naturally wax and wane from day to day, keep showing up. Don't believe or give credence to the critical inner voice that incessantly questions your path or attempts to dissuade you from it. Change your habits if necessary. Question past ways of doing things. Revise and fine-tune your motivation and your approach. But do not give up.

But also remember that the intention behind your action is more important than the form of the action. So don't worry so much about what medium of expression to choose. Just choose. Then channel your inner passion and purpose into that external form. Make it your mission to offer your gifts to the world with love, regardless of any unforeseen obstacles or momentary impediments.

Persist in your purpose. Sometimes there is a light to follow in the darkness. Other times, you must generate that light yourself. Do so now. Emanate your gorgeous radiance and light your way, even through the darkest of nights.

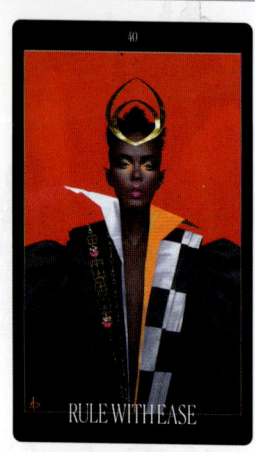

OWN ALL YOUR POWER.

40. RULE WITH EASE

Gather up your dominance. Be a fierce and formidable witch. Lean into your authority and wield it with ease.

As queen of your world, you need not bluster or beg. You can simply acknowledge what you require, desire, and deserve. Then, you can relax and allow yourself to receive.

Be honest with yourself if you are trying too hard and operating from a place of worry or lack. Know that if so, all that is required is an inner shift. Consciously relax, breathe, and remind yourself that you are the ultimate ruler of your realm.

Every good queen knows that if you can't fight a foe, your best option is to become its ally.

So make an alliance with the present moment. Strategically choose to believe that everything that is already happening is working for you, rather than against you. And that no one else holds the authority to take away your power or subtract from your joy.

Once you have allied with the present moment, which holds and embodies the entire cosmos, nothing can stop you. So decide what you want to experience moving forward. Feel it as if it's already present. Celebrate it. Expand into it. And then expect it to naturally, easily, flow on in.

This is also a time to elevate your status in your own eyes. Being respectful of others never needs to involve being relegated to a lower position or rank. Even if someone is an elder in your family or community, or holds a position of authority over you, they are not superior to you. And they are never entitled to demean, belittle, or take advantage of you. In all the ways that matter, you are still their equal. Respectfully acknowledge established dynamics without settling for any kind of mistreatment or abuse.

Gaze at this vampire fae closely. Let her essence be your essence. Internalize her obvious ease with her own authority. Absorb the bright scarlet hue that surrounds her into your aura. Trust your regal status. Emanate your beauty. Sense your shining, golden crown.

BEAUTIFUL NIGHTMARE

41. BEAUTIFUL NIGHTMARE

Find the power in fear. Find something to laugh at, even in the gravest struggle. Breathe into the terror and let it teach you.

Winter follows summer, just as we can rely on night to descend. For every happy daydream, there is a nightmare of heartache or dread. Without the darkness, we would rest fitfully, and have no name for the light.

Optimism is helpful in some cases, but not all. When you attempt to bypass painful and complex feelings, you do yourself no favors. Suppressed emotions do not disappear; they only fester while keeping you disconnected and stuck.

DIVE INTO THE NIGHTMARE.

It is a vital aspect of our mission to give form and outlet to heartbreak and rage. As we channel and transform our human sisters' silence, injustice, and past pain, we take the shape of gorgeous, dangerous femme fatales of the night. Similarly, if you choose to transcend your fear of your own feelings, even your sadness and anger can manifest as radiant splendor and searing power.

You can open to the full spectrum of feeling by playing with darker imagery, symbols, legends, and myths. For example, during the bubonic plague, doctors wore elaborate masks with long beaks, believing the herbs and other ingredients stuffed within would prevent them from contracting the illness themselves. To this day, masqueraders wear masks with long beaks, stirring up your long-buried ancestral memory and collective terror. Once this old fear rises to the surface, it is mingled with celebration, aired out with humor, and converted into a form of play.

Similarly, do not shy away from dark comedy and gallows humor. You will not escape this life without your share of injustice and tragedy. Finding lightness in the bleakest moments is a healing modality that will serve you well.

Never banish a nightmare. Instead, let it assist you in facing your fears and transmuting your heartache. This is a secret to immense and lasting power.

SAVOR THE PLEASURE OF ABSOLUTE COURAGE.

42. A GOOD DAY TO DIE

Be perfectly willing to face this challenge, and every challenge to follow. Summon all the audacity. Go all in.

There is a saying that is often attributed to Native American cultures: "It's a good day to die." In other words, there is nothing I can't face. I'm prepared to act on my convictions and fight for my passionate belief. I am living fully, and enjoying every moment, so I am transcending all fear.

Embrace this philosophy now. Be ready for anything. Don't let false stories or limiting beliefs hold you back. Know your values, state your intentions, put yourself out there, and act in alignment with who you are.

You may fail if you try, but if you don't try, you will certainly never succeed. Seeking to avoid vulnerability will cause you to stagnate. Staying locked in your comfort zone is not courage, but fear. And if you fail, will learn something that will serve you when you try again. So overcome inertia, be proactive, and learn as you go.

We want you to know that you deserve respect and every wonderful thing. So don't hide, shrink, or diminish yourself in the eyes of the world. Don't give your power away to any person, group, or organization. Say yes to your destiny and say no to any arrangement that doesn't feel right to you or provide you with what you require. While you may choose to negotiate or collaborate, don't make a concession that compromises your authority or vision.

Passionately put it all on the line. Know what you value so you can pursue it and defend it. Be the hero you've been waiting for.

43. THE END IS THE BEGINNING

FROM THE RUINS, NEW POWER SPRINGS. SURRENDER TO THE UNKNOWN, ENJOY THE SUSPENSE, AND ACTIVATE THE POTENT MAGIC OF THIS TRANSFORMATIONAL TIME.

When everything falls apart, or when you choose to dismantle one or more of the structures that seem to define your life experience, you stand at a portal of power.

Invisible forces will come to your aid when you let go of apprehension and embrace possibility. This will take you from fear to flow, and in turn, call in a glorious future.

IN DESTRUC-TION, THERE IS POTENTIAL.

Whatever has been demolished is making way for new dreams to coalesce in the ether and manifest into form.

Take some quiet time alone to unclench your jaw, let your shoulders fall away from your ears, and breathe. When you feel calm and present, write a list of your intentions and goals for the future. What would you like to experience? In what ways would you like to succeed? How would you like your life to look? And, most importantly, how will you feel when these wishes are fulfilled? See if you can feel those feelings now. Ask yourself: "What if these intentions were already manifested? How would I feel?" Bring that feeling into your body and mind. Playfully pull it out of the future and into the now.

There is one other vital component to the magic: Let universal power and energy flow in. You may not know just how the world will shape itself to match your inner vision, but the cosmos does. And it is a part of you, just as you are a part of it. So fine-tune your vision, feel the joy associated with your most beautiful future, and invoke the help of the Infinite Consciousness and Divine Presence. Then let go and let flow. You will be amazed by what happens next.

Fear becomes excitement when you release your connection to the past and courageously dive into the unknowable future. Uncertainty comes with exhilaration when you let go of the need to foresee and control.

The past is gone, but the future is wide open before you. Expect miracles, trust your magic, and know that unseen forces are on your side. Uncommon blessings are in store.

44. WELCOME THE STORM

FEEL AND HEAL. YOUR HEART IS HEAVY WITH PAIN. FEEL IT, BREATHE INTO IT, AND LET IT FLOW.

When you deny or stifle your grief, you will feel frustrated, disconnected, and stuck. But when you acknowledge it, breathe into it, and allow it to be, it will begin to heal. In time, it will dissipate and disperse, and you will rediscover the fullness of your joy.

You may feel that if you allow your sorrow to flow, it will drown you. But it won't. While it's true that grief cannot be rushed, it's also true that emotions are not permanent. They are just waves of energy passing through. Breathe,

EMOTION SHALL OVERWHELM BUT NOT OVERTAKE.

relax, and allow them to move. Eventually, they will certainly pass.

You may not be cognizant of the inner pain that is present. It's possible that you have hidden it so thoroughly that its origin is not presently accessible. Whether or not this is the case, you can soften your defenses and make friends with your feelings through the simple practice of conscious breathing.

Gently, persistently, notice as you breathe in and out. As you do this, place one hand on your heart and one hand on your belly as you send yourself love and support through your touch. When you notice your mind has wandered from the breath, simply bring it back. Stay with this practice for as long as it takes. Eventually, your inner barriers will melt, and you will let yourself feel.

Whatever feelings you discover within—yearning, anger, regret, whatever—welcome them. This storm will pass, but first it must rage.

45. ALCHEMY

Dissolve and reform. Transform one condition into another. Channel an old challenge toward creating something constructive and new.

If you are emerging from a past trauma, heal up stronger and more powerful than you were before. If you've encountered a hardship, create art out of it, or use it to inform your future in an empowering way.

The spiritual art of alchemy has a motto: *Solve et coagula*, which means "dissolve and reform."

Let go of the old, honor all it taught you, and sense the raw potential in the wide, open field that it once occupied. Then, reformulate.

Alchemy is the way of existence. After death, there is

TRANSMUTE, REFORMULATE, AND REINVENT.

decay. Decay becomes the fertile soil from which new life springs.

With every breath, we inhale oxygen and exhale carbon dioxide in an endless dance of reciprocal respiration with plants and trees.

Spiraling galaxies come into being, and eventually burn out and disperse, their raw materials first scattering far and wide and then, in different combinations, forming themselves into brand-new solar systems and worlds.

We ourselves were created out of aching sorrow and soul-crushing rage. Now we use that same energy to inspire, guide, protect, and defend.

In your life, too, you can observe the alchemical process at work. For example, you may sense loved ones on the other side who are still with you, guiding you and teaching you, although they have changed since they have left behind their physical form.

Blessings have emerged even from your most grievous problems. Once you got through them, you mined their wisdom and made it a part of your very self.

Now, too, one form is dissolving and another is being born. Make this process conscious. Notice what is changing — what you're letting go of and what you're calling in. Then swirl and gather like stardust — form into a galaxy both beautiful and new.

What will you build in the wasteland? From the ashes of your past, how will you rekindle your fire? What new structures will you construct out of the dust?

46. QUEEN

ACCEPT THE CROWN.
ACKNOWLEDGE YOUR SUCCESS.
RECOGNIZE AND CELEBRATE THE
NEW LEVEL OF MASTERY YOU HAVE
UNLOCKED.

It's been a long and arduous path, requiring focus, courage, and sacrifice. You could have taken an easier and more comfortable road, but you didn't. You set your sights high, and then you committed and persevered. And now you have succeeded.

We see this, and we are proud. We want you to see it too, and to feel pride on your own behalf.

The success to which this card points may be obvious. You may have received a promotion, mastered a skill, or completed a course of study. But this message may be about a less tangible milestone, such as healing your heart after a breakup, gaining

HAIL THE QUEEN.

the confidence to speak up about something important to you, moving to a new city where you didn't know anyone, or otherwise triumphing over inertia and fear.

Whatever your achievement may be, name it. Don't minimize it or take it for granted. Don't laugh it off or explain it away. And certainly don't deny it or behave as if you can't possibly imagine what it is. Define, name, and claim your success. Then, congratulate yourself for it and be pleased.

Being queen is about ruling your world, sure. But it's also about simply experiencing the joy of your own regal authority. You're powerful. You're magical. You're brave. And you've come so far. Give yourself a gift as a token of self-appreciation. Do at least one tangible thing to observe this milestone. Throw a party, light a candle, or bake a cake.

A well-lived life is, in many ways, a constant evolution. But you must not get so carried away with self-cultivation that you forget to stop, revel in your accomplishments, and enjoy how magnificent you already are.

ASSASSIN

SLAY THE SABOTEUR.

47. ASSASSIN

Kill the inner critic. Refuse to tolerate the detrimental internal voice. Move forward with masterful efficiency, and don't look back.

There is a voice within you that is not you. It is a voice of shame, fear, comparison, and self-loathing that you have internalized through your exposure to a disempowering relationship pattern or bogus cultural narrative.

This inner contingency may tear you down with words or feelings of crippling shame, body negativity, free-floating anxiety, or general fear.

Show no mercy as you swiftly put an end to this critical voice's grisly reign.

Look deeply and see clearly. You know who you are and who you aren't. And you aren't the mean voice that tells you awful things that you don't even believe. You would never ever speak that way to another person. So instead of giving that voice another ounce of your precious attention, kill it now. Slay it swiftly, expertly, and without remorse.

The critical voice will try to convince you that you need it because it helps keep you in line. But this isn't true. Abuse doesn't serve any practical purpose. It just holds you back and keeps you scared. In fact, you will learn better, and feel better, when you treat yourself with kindness and respect.

Set the intention to be yourself, fully and without apology, and to love and approve of who you are. Also be aware that the critical inner voice may arise in various forms throughout your lifetime. But whenever you notice it, you can assassinate it again. You can simply, unswervingly refuse to allow it to have power over you.

All that is needed is an inner shift, and that inner shift will be easier than you might expect. You will be surprised how easy it is to kill the voice that has previously seemed so fearsome. In fact, it's nothing. Nothing at all. So, you will kill it when you send it back to the nothingness that is its native state.

You slay the saboteur when you assert your authority, both within and without. You kill the inner critic when you remember it's not your job to please or impress everyone (and it's impossible anyway). Your life is for you, not for making others comfortable or for chasing after imaginary and inauthentic standards.

STEADFAST PROTECTOR

CHAMPION YOUR CAUSE.

48. STEADFAST PROTECTOR

FIGHT FOR WHAT YOU CARE ABOUT. LIVE IN INTEGRITY. NAME, CLAIM, AND STAUNCHLY DEFEND YOUR VALUES.

Ask, and we will happily share our fierceness with you, and teach you to make it your own. Channel that power toward standing up for and protecting what is precious to you. Guard it with your life and never give up.

Ask yourself: "What do I value? What motivates me — in my work, my spirituality, my relationships, and my life? What is sacred to me? Who and what would I fight to the death to protect?"

In addition to knowing what you care about and desire to protect, it will help you to make a list of your core values, and to distill them into a single word or phrase. Let this act as your guiding star as you move through your present challenge.

There are times when politeness and inaction are not ethical. For example, you must not stand idly by while others are mistreated. You must not allow Mother Earth to be even more injured than she already is. You must not hide your passionate convictions to stay popular or keep the peace. Doing what is right often demands sacrifice and risk. Make it a core value to never hesitate to do what you know in your heart is right.

Don't let others shame you for speaking out angrily about unfairness, atrocity, or your own mistreatment. There is no virtue in pretending to be okay with what is not okay. And there is often great virtue in making a terrible fuss.

When you get clear on, and live by, your values, you will be an unstoppable force. You will help others while channeling all your wisdom, knowledge, and expertise into bringing your immaculate inner visions into form.

THE FUTURE IS BRIGHT.

49. A NEW DAY

EXPAND YOUR WORLD. EXPECT A MIRACLE. AFTER A DARK NIGHT, A NEW DAY IS DAWNING OR ABOUT TO DAWN.

Look upon the horizon with joy. For immense blessings are in store.

We see every human life is an alchemical process. You are always dissolving and reforming, transforming from one state to another. Whether you do this with consciousness and deliberate intention or you do it by default, you and your life conditions are forever in flux. But the most extraordinary lives are lived by those who cocreate with the universe to formulate the changes they desire.

It could be that you have been going through a dark night of the soul, and you are finally beginning to see the dawn. But even when you have succeeded in crafting the life of your dreams, there is always more to experience: new possibilities to discover, new worlds to explore, and even more lavish and expansive blessings to call in.

This is good news. Smile to it. Energetically expand into it. Know that no matter how many times you have been frustrated, hurt, or disappointed in the past, your most ideal life conditions are indeed in the ether, and are even now gathering momentum and coagulating into form.

Channel this positive potential powerfully by clarifying your goals and desires. Write them out, in the present tense, as if already 100% real and true. Then feel the pleasurable emotions connected to them. Celebrate these conditions and feel grateful for them, as if they are already there in your life experience now. Each day, look for them and joyfully expect to see them in the perfect time and way.

Welcome to this gorgeous new day. Revel in it. Embrace it. Notice every blessing, little and big, and dare to believe that you are entitled to endless moments of success and delight.

LOOK DEEPLY AND SEE.

50. ASK AND KNOW

OPEN TO GUIDANCE. ASK FOR THE ANSWER OR ANSWERS YOU SEEK. THEN RELAX, LOOK DEEPLY, AND ALLOW YOURSELF TO KNOW.

Here you see a vampire faerie who is in love with a human who has been away on a quest. She is concerned that she has received no communications from him and wonders why he has not yet returned. Tired of waiting and wondering, she has decided to scry: to gaze into the sacred pond and ask the powers that be to show her what she needs to know.

You have already begun to search for answers by consulting the oracle and drawing this card. Now look even further — not just within the words you read here, but also within your own awareness: the still, quiet depths of your soul. There you will find the truth you need to see. Close your eyes, breathe, calm your mind, and expect to receive an image, word, phrase, feeling, or calm inner knowing that will shed light into the darkness and exchange uncertainty for clarity.

Follow your intuition about any additional ritual aspects that will assist you in discovering what you want and need to know. For example, you might light a candle and let your eyes rest on a crystal ball, take a walk in nature while contemplating your question, or pose your inquiry before bed and be ready to jot down any dreams you remember when you awake.

Or try simply writing your question at the top of a blank page, and then free-write whatever words come through in response. There is something about the act of taking a pen to paper that brings forth answers that are already there for you, but that have previously been hidden or obscured.

However you choose to draw upon your deep inner wisdom and the wisdom of the Infinite, this card is a sure sign that you have access to the knowledge and guidance you desire.

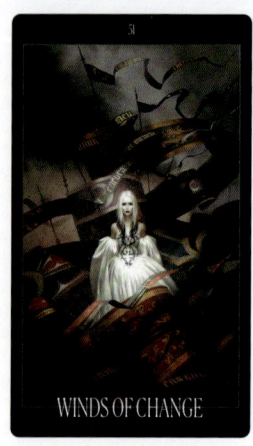

51. WINDS OF CHANGE

You and your life conditions are undergoing profound and multilayered changes. Surrender to this process. Brave the discomfort and see what transpires.

THIS CHANGE IS FOR THE BEST.

This card has appeared to shore up your perseverance as you face these mighty winds of change. Believe us when we tell you this time of upheaval won't last forever, and know that the changes you are experiencing will ultimately prove to be positive. Soon, the winds will abate, the dust will settle, and you'll be able to see where you stand.

Even though the clarity provided by stable serenity may feel out of reach, know that you are evolving, learning, and gaining greater mastery over your world. While some inner and outer structures are dissolving and falling away, they are making room for other, more aligned and supportive structures to appear.

You can traverse this transformational time in the most harmonious possible way by taking care of yourself as best you can. Even though your schedule might seem to be overly full as it is, do your best to carve out even a little bit of time each day for meditation, quiet alone time, communing with nature, or ritual self-care such as baths and beauty treatments.

If, in the past, you've been through trauma of any kind, don't minimize it or explain it away through comparison or self-blame. Inwardly recognize how hard it was, and compassionately acknowledge any lingering effects. Remember that the trauma and its effects are not your fault; take care of yourself as needed, and offer yourself kindness and love.

Tumultuous winds of change—unsettled, unmoored, rapidly shifting feelings and conditions—blow into every life at one time or another. But they won't stay forever. They will pass through, topple old regimes, clear the air, and push you to heal and expand. And then they will move on.

EYE OF THE STORM

IN SERENITY, THERE IS FIERCENESS.

52. EYE OF THE STORM

WIELD INNER TRANQUILITY. BE UNRUFFLED AND COMPOSED. KNOW THAT YOU ARE SAFE.

At the center of a cyclone, the weather is calm. In the middle of battle, this vampire fae is confident. For this is far from her first.

Enchanted and impermeable, her armor has become a part of her very being. Following her body's wisdom and clear inner guidance, she sits relaxed, channeling any frenetic or excess energy down through her sword and hands into the earth. Ready for anything, and secure in her swiftness and hard-won expertise, she waits, trusting she will know just when to act.

Similarly, this is not your first battle. You have been through challenges before, and always emerged stronger, wiser, and with deeper insight and skill. Even though life requires improvisation and swift spontaneity, you are prepared. Brandish your own relaxed proficiency. Let go of worry and allow your actions to be guided by your well-honed mastery and the exquisitely honed compass within.

Your mind inhabits your entire body, and your spirit, and even the subtle connections with the earth and other living things. When you believe your mind lives only in your brain, and that it must foresee every contingency and micromanage all the possible details, your thinking becomes like ungrounded electricity that burns out and fritters away.

Meditation, conscious movement, and relaxation exercises can help you allow your consciousness to inhabit your entire body and sensitize to the subtle fluctuations in your environment and the outside world. Practice one or more of these things daily to expertly wield the sword of calm that will allow you to survive, thrive, and—inevitably—triumph.

Photo © Whitney DeVoto / @devotophoto

ABOUT THE AUTHOR

TESS WHITEHURST BELIEVES LIFE IS MAGICAL. In addition to authoring this deck, she's the author of *The Wild Witch Oracle*, *The Tarot of Secrets*, *The Halloween Forever Oracle*, *The Oracle of Daydreams and Moonbeams*, *The Oracle of Portals*, *Cosmic Dancer Oracle*, *The Queen Mab Oracle*, *The Magic of Flowers Oracle*, and *The Angel Magic Oracle*.

Tess's books include the bestselling *Magical Housekeeping*, *Radiant: Embracing Your Power and Beauty at Midlife*, and lots of other fan favorites such as *You Are Magical*, *The Good Energy Book*, and *The Magic of Flowers*. Articles she has written have appeared in *Writer's Digest*, *Spirit & Destiny*, and *Llewellyn's Magical Almanac*. She has appeared on morning shows on both Fox and NBC, and her feng shui work was featured on the Bravo TV show *Flipping Out*.

Tess's teachings about magic and spirituality appear extensively online, particularly on her website, and via her online membership portal, Wisdom Circle Online School of Magical Arts.

Tess lives in the Central Valley of California with a handsome man and a handsome cat.

Visit Tess and sign up for her free newsletter at **TessWhitehurst.com**.

ABOUT THE ARTIST

MÉLANIE DELON IS A FREELANCE ILLUSTRATOR who lives in a small town near Alençon (Normandy, France). She creates illustrations for book covers, has worked for many publishing houses around the world, and has created concept art for the video game industry. Mélanie also has a number of works in progress for magazines specializing in 2D.

In 2007, Mélanie published her first art book, *Elixir 1* — a collection of illustrations with short stories, followed by the second volume in 2010. The worlds Mélanie seeks to create through her illustrations are based on fantasy—her favorite subject—but she always adds a touch of classicism and romanticism, as she finds mixing styles brings more realism to the painting.

After studying History of Art and Archeology at the Sorbonne, Mélanie went to a 3D school where she discovered digital illustration. She started to work as a freelance illustrator in 2005 by trading her pens and paper for Photoshop and a Wacom graphic tablet.

In 2012, Mélanie opened her own publishing house/shop, EXUVIA. In 2014, she released her third art book, *Opale 1*, under this label. The second volume was released in 2023.

Mélanie has taught digital painting at CGMA since 2017.

www.melaniedelon.com

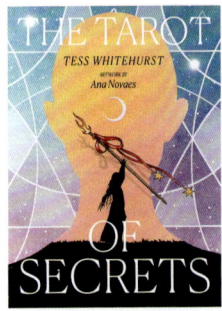

THE TAROT OF SECRETS
A formulary, catalyst, and key

Tess Whitehurst
Artwork by Ana Novaes

There are secrets here. Deep secrets. Timeless secrets to connect you with a formidable current of universal wisdom and renovate your world.

The secrets are within you, just as they are in the soil, the clouds, the oceans, and the stars.

The Tarot of Secrets, from renowned author Tess Whitehurst, offers the formula to unlock and embody these mysteries through your own transcendent DNA. Artist Ana Novaes re-imagines Tarot for the 21st century, weaving together traditional esoteric symbolism and everyday experience to produce an evocative deck that will be loved by novices and collectors alike.

Ask questions. Look for answers. Contemplate the images and let the words speak to you. Approach this deck with the earnest desire of the Magician, the patient focus of the High Priestess, and the limitless enthusiasm of the Fool.

Internalize the knowledge of the alchemists that echoes through the halls of eternity. Transmute the tin of your everyday experience and the lead of life's challenges into a fountain of spiritual gold.

78 cards + 352-page colour guidebook.
ISBN: 978-1-922574-45-9

THE WILD WITCH ORACLE
Shapeshifters, Rebels & Queens

Tess Whitehurst
Artwork by Tammy Wampler

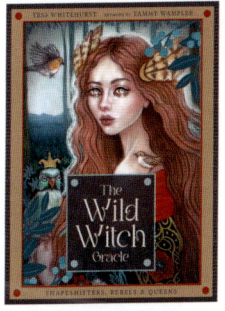

The brave spirits of this deck—the queens, shapeshifters, and rebels—are here to call you back to your native wildness: to remind you that you are wise, independent, empowered, and free.

Featuring 44 bold heroines voiced by author Tess Whitehurst and beautifully illustrated by artist Tammy Wampler, *The Wild Witch Oracle* delivers messages that enliven your courage to create a life that's truly authentic.

From astrological goddesses to nature sprites, faerie queens to historical monarchs, the supernatural and the human collide, awakening your innate divine powers.

What do you yearn for? Feel into your question and draw a card. These feminine role models will respond with practical guidance to shake up the status quo and reclaim your rightful inheritance — your primordial power and unique magic.

44 cards + 160-page colour guidebook.
ISBN: 978-1-922574-39-8

THE QUEEN MAB ORACLE
Divine Feminine Wisdom from the Queen of the Fae

Tess Whitehurst
Artwork by Mélanie Delon & Cecilia G.F.

From all such stuff that dreams are made of ...

... even now, answers are on the way to you. On the wings of an endless midsummer's night, something blessed this way comes, powered by the earth, the wind and the divine radiance of the Faery Queen.

Ancient and powerful, Queen Mab is an elemental emissary of charm, moonlight and manifestation. Turn to her for meaning, revelation and insight into the poetry and empowerment at play within all that is and all you shall become.

"Queen Mab, I hear and embody your wisdom so that I may own my divinity and affirm magic in the world."

45 cards + 160-page colour guidebook.
ISBN: 978-1-922573-77-3

THE HALLOWEEN FOREVER ORACLE

Tess Whitehurst
Artwork by Jasmine Becket-Griffith

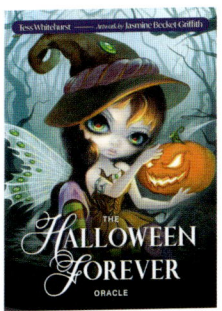

Step into *The Halloween Forever Oracle*, where the veil between worlds is perpetually thin. Drawing inspiration from traditions like Samhain and Día de los Muertos, this oracle offers year-round guidance and answers from the realms of spirit and magic.

Featuring the artwork of world-renowned Jasmine Becket-Griffith and the whimsical words of Tess Whitehurst, these cards invite you to embrace the eerie and enchanting as you unveil the keys to happiness, personal power and healing.

A glow-in-the-dark party awaits you. Let ghostly laughter guide you as trick-or-treaters knock on your door, enticing you into a journey of self-discovery. Dare to embrace the shadows and explore the depths of your soul in this delightfully secret and spooky realm, where every day is Halloween.

46 cards + 112-page colour guidebook.
ISBN: 978-1-922574-17-6

For more information on this
or any Blue Angel Publishing release,
please visit our website at:

WWW.BLUEANGELONLINE.COM